DIY HOMEMADE MEDICAL FACE MASK

Step by Step Guide on How to Make your Medical Face Mask with Filter Pocket, Face-Mask, Protective Mask, Washable Mask, Face Mask At Home To Protect You From Virus

@JennyRobbins

Copyright 2020 All rights reserved.

This document is geared towards providing exact and reliable information in regards to the topic and issue covered. The publication is sold with the idea that the publisher is not required to render accounting, officially permitted, or otherwise, qualified services. If advice is necessary, legal or professional, a practiced individual in the profession should be ordered. - From a Declaration of Principles which was accepted and approved equally by a Committee of the American Bar Association and a Committee of Publishers and Associations. In no way is it legal to reproduce, duplicate, or transmit any part of this document in either electronic means or in printed format. Recording of this publication is strictly prohibited and any storage of this document is not allowed unless with written permission from the publisher. All rights reserved. The information provided herein is stated to be truthful and consistent, in that any liability, in terms of inattention or otherwise, by any usage or abuse of any policies, processes, or directions contained within is the solitary and utter responsibility of the recipient reader. Under no circumstances will any legal responsibility or blame be held against the publisher for any reparation, damages, or monetary loss due to the information herein, either directly or indirectly. Respective authors own all copyrights not held by the publisher. The information herein is offered for informational purposes solely, and is universal as so. The presentation of the information is without contract or any type of guarantee assurance. The trademarks that are used are without any consent, and the publication of the trademark is without permission or backing by the trademark owner. All trademarks and brands within this book are for clarifying purposes only and are the owned by the owners themselves, not affiliated with this document.

TABLE OF CONTENTS

INTRODUCTION 1

CHAPTER 1: HOME-MADE FACE MASKS 4

CHAPTER 2: IMPORTANCE OF MAKING YOUR OWN FACE MASK 8

CHAPTER 3: ARE DIY FACE MASKS EFFECTIVE AND ACCEPTABLE? 15

CHAPTER 4: PATTERN AND PROCEDURE FOR DIY HOMEMADE MASKS 19

CHAPTER 5: DIY FACE MASKS USAGE 26

CHAPTER 6: MEDICAL PROTECTIVE MASKS (AKA N95, KN95 MASKS) 29

CHAPTER 7: DIY FABRIC FACE MASKS REQUIREMENTS 33

CHAPTER 8: FABRIC FACE MASK PATTERNS 35

CHAPTER 9: HOW TO SEW A SURGICAL FACE MASK 38

CHAPTER 10: STEPS FOR SEWING A FABRIC HOSPITAL MASK 41

CHAPTER 11: HOMEMADE FACEMASK PATTERNS 48

CHAPTER 12: WHEN ARE YOU SUPPOSED TO WEAR A FACE MASK? 51

CONCLUSION 55

INTRODUCTION

Homemade facial masks are highly recommended for the prevention of virus. Home-made facial masks and face coatings are now approved to wear in public, from the hand-sewn tissues to bandanas and rubber bands.

Late last week, the Centers for Disease Control and Prevention released a revised guide to the public's wearing of facial covers, including home-made fabric masks. The updated statement comes as cases in the US and new data about VIRUS transmission are published.

For months, the CDC has advised people suspected or confirmed ill with the VIRUS to use medical-grade facial masks as well as emergency care staff. But spiking cases in the United States and especially in hotspots such as New York and Now New Jersey have shown that current policies are not powerful enough to flatten the curve.

There are also new evidence that a home-made mask can be used in crowded areas such as the supermarket, against no face cover at all. Significant attention is also paid to social distancing and hand washing.

The use of the masks by all people can provide some barrier protection against respiratory droplets coughed or sneezed around. Early reports indicate that the virus can spend up to one to three hours in the air after an infected person leaves the area. Covering the skin helps to keep these droplets from reaching and infecting others.

According to the American Lung Association, one in every four people diagnosed with VIRUS may show mild or zero symptoms at all.

When you are around others, using a cloth face mask will help trap large particles that could be expelled through a tingling, sneezing, or accidentally began saliva (e.g. by speaking), which may delay transmission to others if you are not sure you are sick.

The American Lung Association says in a blog post that addresses the wearing of homemade masks, 'these masks are not intended to shield the wearer, but to defend it against accidental transmission – in case you are an Asymptomatic Carrier of Virus.

The most important thing about the CDC message is that it is a 'voluntary public health measure' to cover your face on your way home and should not replace proven precautions, such as self-quarantine at home, social distances and hand washing thoroughly.

I hope and pray that manufacturers will be able to manufacture the medical grade face masks that are required by our health professionals! Meanwhile, making home-made facial masks as a last resort is one little thing that I can do to help during this tough time.

This GUIDE explores step by step guide on how to make your medical face mask with filter pocket, face-mask, protective mask, washable mask, face mask at home to protect you from virus.

Let's get started.

CHAPTER 1: Home-Made Face Masks

From a medical standpoint, dust, bacteria, viruses and various harmful gasses are found in air which can enter through the nose, pharynx, trachea, which lungs through human breathing.

Wearing a disposable face mask ensures that the respiratory tract is "barred" in order to allow the inhaled air to absorb and avoid bacteria and viruses from entering the body. Around the same time, a mask can also protect the mouth and nose from wearing bacteria and viruses.

Wearing a disposable face mask can also reduce or prevent dust stimulation of the respiratory tract that can prevent or reduce occupational diseases. Anti-virus masks should be used in workplaces with toxic and harmful particular odors to avoid occupational diseases triggered by inhalation of toxic and harmful gasses, such as benzene toxicity and organic solvent toxicity.

The uses of Surgical Masks today go far beyond the medical and health care field in response to public concern. The epidemic of infectious diseases such as influenza has sparked a rising market for face masks. However, studies indicate that standard masks do not provide adequate protection since microbe-bearing particles can easily go through them.

Recently, surgical mask manufacturers have been working hard to create a face mask form called "respirator" Their security is much higher, since the stringent filter has a germicide that disinfects all products including microbes. They are used both domestically and globally in millions of medical departments, hospitals and clinics.

N99 Surgical respiratory machines with screening glue have a much higher antimicrobial protection than standard N95 masks that hold an elastic band in the nose.

The prevalence of airborne diseases and pathogens is no longer a mystery. Whether it is, H1N1 or avian flu virus or others virus, the long-term survival plan involves first and foremost shielding people from respiratory infections.

There are concerns among health professionals that, when a microbe evolves, a highly infectious airborne infection will spread every day to the general public. Today, as in 1918, the devastating Spanish flu pandemic has killed an estimated 50 million people, this possibility remains.

N99 Respirators are usually latex-free in their looks and have a much tighter mesh that removes almost all airborne products. They often close holes across the nose and facial sides.

This adhesive does not allow air to be inhaled when the N99 grade filter passes. This is super quick to breathe and should be taken into account when planning for any pandemic.

For this purpose, surgical masks with a bacterial efficacy of 99 percent or higher are recommended for preparation for such an outbreak. Among other things, medical gloves, hand sanitizers and other products are required to keep the area safe and sterile. Taking these precautions is the safest way to prevent airborne disease transmission.

Surgical masks are an effective way to protect people from respiratory diseases. One must, however, be aware of the most appropriate types of masks, as not all are the same.

The Centers for Disease Control and Prevention (CDC) has now recommended that everyone wear cloth-side masks like home-made masks, even in public places where it is difficult to keep 6 feet away from others, in order to prevent the spread of virus from individuals without symptoms.

In addition to continuous social isolation and good hygiene procedures, this suggestion is highly recommended.

Healthcare workers should be particularly careful when using home-made facial masks. These masks should be used preferably in conjunction with a face shield which covers the whole face and side and extends to or below the chin.

Benefit from handmade facial masks

The facial masks can be made from ordinary materials at home and there is limitless provision.

This will reduce the risk of people transmitting the virus without symptoms by speaking, coughing or sneezing.

These are better than not using a mask and provide protection, particularly where isolation from society is difficult to maintain.

Risks of homemade facial masks

They can offer a false sense of health. Although homemade facial masks provide some kind of protection, they are much less protective than surgical masks or respirators.

These will not eliminate or raising the need for additional protections. Proper hygiene and social isolation are still the best ways to remain healthy.

CHAPTER 2: Importance Of Making Your Own Face Mask

Many people shop for surgical masks to protect themselves against this deadly disease with extremely infectious of vurus spread rapidly across the world.

The rapid increase in demand for "Personal Protective Equipment" (PPE) and disrupted supply lines across China resulted in a serious shortage in small particulate filtering face masks (N-95s).

News reports, which were properly intended to reserve for medical institutions limited supplies of these disposable items, asked people not to buy such items. Public officials have been quoted to suggest – incorrectly – that face coverings cannot help prevent this new virus from spreading.

The truth is more complicated: virus spreads from person to person in outlets of humidity, mucus and saliva from infected people. These virus particles are brought into the air through coughing, sneezing and even regular breathing. Thousands of outlets can be removed by a sneeze.

These virus particles may be coated by people less than 6 feet away and still in the air. Following droplets, the particles of the virus can remain active for up to nine days.

Infection happens when someone breathes in the infectious droplets, or when the hands coated in virus particles that fall out of air onto the shelves, rails of the hand, the floor or other surface contact their mouth, nose or eyes.

A DIY mask is not a perfect substitute for a professional mask, but it can be a decent alternative. For a time, it seemed like every day healthcare professional advice changed if most Americans had to wear face masks to help prevent the spread of virus.

The Centers for Disease Control and Prevention (CDC) has now formally instructed all but children to wear a cloth mask or facial shield in many public settings.

The practice has already been widely spread in many parts of Asia, which some experts say may be one explanation why places such as Hong Kong and South Korea appeared to contain the virus.

Above all, it is critically critical that medical staff, vulnerable groups and those with the virus are first in line when it comes to medical equipment for personal safety or PPE.

That is why it may be an alternative, even if it does not provide exactly the same degree of security, and probably reduce considerable strain on the already dramatically overloaded supply chain.

Now that you are trapped inside, I am not going to write a sleek and elegant line about how you are likely to have a long time in your hands for art projects, because now you have children, or maybe a job that does not allow you to work from home, or a job that is endlessly stressful now. I am simply a semi-professional crafter and I cannot even hesitate for most days to sit down and knit a few rows.

What I am going to do is answer some questions you may have about making a mask — especially! — if you are not a crafter yourself. If you have specific questions or services, email me to let me know; I am alanna.okun@vox.com, and this guide is likely to be updated regularly as specific information is available.

So wait, should I certainly wear a mask?

What if I am not weak or sick?

The guidance now is that all Americans (except infants) should have some kind of face in public places where other social distance measures are difficult to maintain (like supermarkets or pharmacies), in particular in communities with significant transmission rates.

Virus tends to spread mainly if germ-containing droplets turn it into the mouth, nose, or eyes of aN individual. If your mouth and nose have a physical barrier, it is just less likely. There was a mistake.

Although it shows how many masks are to protect users against virus — because it is not clear if the virus spreads by airborne droplets — masks do not disperse their own droplets.

When you breathe, chat, laugh, sigh, yawn, sneeze, or cough in public, droplets on check-outs, dining tables and everywhere else are less likely to occur when you have a droplet. It could prevent individuals, including asymptomatic ones, from transmitting infection.

The production of a mask is basically not a bad idea, since the buy-in is very small and your chances of owning materials are already very high. You certainly would not have to go out and buy anything new, and if you do, several contact-free or online options are available.

All right, tell me about these materials

There are official instructions from the CDC as to what features of home-made masks such as several layers of tight fitting and machine washing should have. It also recommends which fabrics to look for: "Tightly woven cloth, such as quilting or cloth sheets.

Many of the no-sew videos may not even need to be cut; handkerchiefs, fabric napkins or bandanas may be used in such situations. T-shirts are also used.

The CDC has instructions for a sewn option and two none-sewn alternatives which allow two 10x6 inch fabric rectangles per mask. There is also a helpful step-by-step guide to home-made masks in the New York Times, which can be made with a sewing machine or by hand, and a slightly more involved design for the printing of the right cloth.

One thing to remember is fit and wear — the probability that a handmade mask will not suit you as comfortably as a doctor is higher than a professional mask that reduces its efficacy.

That said, if you do not have any other option, you can wrap a piece of fabric around your nose. The CDC suggests that you wear a face mask in your approach to sick people, One of the strategies recommended by the CDC is to take a t-shirt off so that the face mask fits better.

If you are searching for something half way between those two poles, this tutorial by an online Japanese art and crafts instructor named Japanese Creations shows how you can use a handkerchief (or a scarf or cloth or other fabric) to create an unsewn mask, and how you have hair ties.

The same approach is used for many CDC no-sew processes, for inserting a trimmed coffee filter in a center for additional filtration.

Taking a facial mask protects people from being contaminated in two ways:

1) By removing most virus-filled airborne droplets

(2) by preventing the wearer to contact his own mouth and nose.

Studies showed that a physician who uses surgical facial masks correctly receives 80% less infections than others.

Why the mixed messages, then?

First, because only when the masks are used properly does the protection come. They must be clean, carefully removed and hand-washed, and the practice must not touch the skin.

Secondly, since gaps between masks and fibers are too wide, even in commercial surgical masks, to block all viruses. Sneeze and cough gout typically range from 7 to 100 microns. Surgical masks and other tissue masks are going to block 7 micron particles. The virus particles of virus are 0.06 to 0.14 microns.

Then why are you supposed to make your own face masks?

1) If you get sick, supplies of masks at home will give friends and family some safety when seeking medical advice. This would certainly be better than no mask (see study notes).

2) By making your own, and preferably for family and friends, you can decrease the need for small supplies of imported industrial goods, which hospitals and nursing homes urgently need.

3) These convenient, curved masks rest better than rectangular surgical masks, with less gaps.

4) Our handmade prototypes are washable and eco-friendly.

Furniture:

Mask 1 is mounted with 2 fabric layers and an optional filter pocket between them. That is supported by elastic earrings. Elastic can also be wrapped around the ear.

Mask 2 is fitted and made simpler, with 2 layers but no pocket. Seam allowances are 1⁄4 "(9"x 15" fabric outer layer 9 "x 15" fabric liner layer (the 3 standard or large size masks can be made from 1/4 yard (9) "of 45" long fabric) and approximately 3 "pieces of soft wire (which can either be ornamental wire as shown, or wire, or even a clip if this is all you can find) as specified by the MASK 1 & 2 supplies (child, normal and big): 22 "elastic string (10" kid size length, 11-12 "length, 13" length).

CHAPTER 3: Are DIY Face Masks Effective And Acceptable?

Some of the stories have changed as knowledge about the virus pandemic emerges. For the latest VIRUS information, visit CDC, WHO and your local public health department online resources.

Creating a DIY face mask is the safest residence during the latest virus epidemic – whether for your own personal use or to donate to healthcare facilities. The CDC also suggests that you wear a mask every time you go out.

In addition, medical face masks are dangerously small for health care staff, as VIRUS patients are increasingly increasing and many customers purchased personal protection gear (PPE) to stay at home.

Hospitals are demanding donations of N95 breathers (the CDC masks approved for health professionals working with infected patients). But such measures are not enough to satisfy the demand for N95 masks, so businesses and good Samaritans knit masks to physicians, nurses, and other health-care professionals operating on the front lines of the latest virus.

The supply of PEP has become a crisis such that hospital staff take to social media to call for surgical masks sewn by hand.

Facebook groups, YouTube channels and Instagram pages pop up with craftsmen to find out how to make home-made masks and bring them into the hands of health workers. If you own a sewing machine, you can participate in this campaign, however you first need to learn some important details.

The Good Home keeping Institute Textiles Laboratory has met medical practitioners, sewing experts, and fabric vendors to collect what you need to learn about making face masks, from sewing tips to hospital guidance.

Do face masks of fabric work?

Yes and no. They are not so effective as N95 masks for people in hospitals who handle VIRUS patients. That said, they are still useful because hospitals absolutely lack masks. The CDC recommends the use of N95 masks for the best safety.

Furthermore, it states that the last resort is a bandana or scarf if the licensed masks in the hospital are not available. Unfortunately we are in this pandemic at this stage, so homemade masks are made to replace scarves and bandanas.

The homemade versions are also used on N95 masks for longer duration. These masks are rationed wherever they still exist. Although used for one purpose, hospital workers are told to wear the same N95 mask for days or weeks at a time.

Whether you or someone you know has masks of N95, you are encouraged by hospitals to donate or to sell them. For someone other than health care workers working with patients directly, the CDC does not allow the use of N95 masks.

If you look for a mask for yourself and those who do not treat VIRUS patients, you can use homemade tissue masks to delay virus spread.

Such cloth masks will help you maintain a safe six-foot walk from other shoppers, in locations such as a grocery store or pharmacy. This works better if everyone wears them as the infection can still be transmitted by people who have no symptoms.

What fabric should I use?

The best fabric for handmade masks is a 100% cotton tightly woven fabric. All good choices include bed linen and woven shirts. If you donate masks, I recommend staying away knit fabrics (e.g. T-shirts in a jersey) as they produce gaps while stretching, through which the virus will get in.

Be sure that textiles using hot water are prewashed to destroy germs and the cloth is prewashed so that it does not change its shape after the workers have washed themselves.

I spoke to many medical professionals and it is clear that there are currently no specific guidelines or legislation for the creation of handmade masks for donations. Nonetheless, you should observe some best practices.

In addition, you would need a nonwoven design on top of a sewing machine and fabric to block particles and a metal frame (like a clip on paper) to fit well around the nose.

If you have decent clothes or bedding at home, you can use it instead of having to buy new fabric. You can also call the store to bring supplies into your car to pick up the curbside if you have a sewing machine at home and do not want to enter the store.

Would homemade masks be allowed in hospitals?

Technically, home-made masks are not allowed in hospitals, and some hospitals do not accept the donations directly. Take a look at local hospitals in your area and see if they can use DIY masks and, if so, what their policies are. Because the situation is changing increasingly, hospitals need to change policies.

Otherwise, healthcare workers make social media requests. Keep in mind that not only hospitals require face masks. Healthcare staff in other facilities such as hospitals and emergency care centers also deal with mask shortages when dealing with VIRUS patients.

Only non-health staff such as veterinarians and firefighters have no face masks and claim that they embrace homemade models.

CHAPTER 4: Pattern And Procedure For DIY Homemade Masks

Organizations around the US are using sewerage, sewing machines to help produce homemade masks to tackle the virus shortage.

There is one thing you should learn before you immerse yourself in the debate about masks: the public should not buy surgical masks or respirator N95. Health workers face shortages and require these masks to treat patients with virus.

Face Cover is preferred, but not necessary

Homemade masks do not replace social isolation and staying at home. If you want to make a mask, here are step by step directions – based on guidelines given by the Medical Center Vanderbilt University and the Froedtert & Medical College of Wisconsin.

Before you can sew your cotton, you need the following materials:

- 2 pieces of tight cloth, 9 x 6 cm (per mask) four cloth lines,
- 2 x 16 cm (per mask)
- Needle and thread
- Pencil or Scissors
- A handful of Iron sewing pins

Directions

1. Cut your fabric into two rectangles of 9 x 6 inches. Put them up on each other.

2. Pin or mark a 2-inch gap at the top of the 9-inch side, at the middle of the top edge, between 5.5-inch and 3.5- level, at the top edge. Then sew those edges on the either side where the opening was marked or pinned. You will need the 2-inch opening to turn the mask right.

3. Sew the other three mask faces, too.

4. Turn right through the 2-inch gap on the top left. Then click the iron mask to get rid of the wrinkles.

5. Line the ruler up on the six-inch side of the mask vertically. From 1.5-inch line, you can pin where you are going to cut your plugs on your hand. These plugs help to extend the mask. Add the 3-, 2-, 3.5-, 4.5- and 5-inch rows again.

6. Bring the pin down to the level of 2 inches on the 1.5 inch side, and here you made a pleat! Repeat the 3-inch versus 3.5-inch and 4.5-inch versus 5-inch version. Place the new pleats on the other side and repeat.

7. Sew up the sides of your mask so that the platters are smooth.

Render links to the mask

1. Split four fabric strips, 2 inches wide and 16 inches long.

2. Fold them in half the longitudinal direction.

3. Place them on the long side under 1/4-inch.

4. Stitch them in place and then shut the long leg.

5. Add each attachment to a mask corner.

6. Sew again around the edge of the mask and add the ties — so you have finished your mask now.

DIY Face Mask Surgical Pattern

This DIY face mask surgical pattern is free of 3 variations!

When separated or quarantined, 3 ways to make a medical facial mask to remove germs and knit something positive are available! This chapter will also help you to find a homegrown pandemic mask donation room.

There is proof that such masks do NOT work and that PPE masks do not work, and there is a debate as to whether or not they are required. For cases like a pandemic anything is better than none and handmade masks should be worn according to CDC's Crisis Capacity Strategies.

I hope these masks do not stop in the pandemic front, but I hope they do release masks from other fields of healthcare so that the surgical masks of a medical level can be used in the treatment of VIRUS patients.

Ways to make a DIY surgical face mask

1ST VARIATION

1. Cut two lengths 1/4" elastic 14".
2. Pin one length at the top and one at the bottom of the fabric. Face down the second piece of cloth.

3. Sew both borders with a 1/4″ seam permissibility, leaving a slight gap to transform. Turn, click and make pattern-by-piece pleats.

4. Place down and backstitch button pleats. This stitching often covers the left gap.

5. Cut two squares from the pattern and sew together with the right hand.

2ND VARIATION

Using a 1/4 "seam supply inside, so that a slight opening turns to one side.

Turn right and click. Turn right. Then click 3/8″ and stitch in place on both hands. Thread 7″ round elastic through opening with a large stick / yarn needle. Fasten the elastic.

Flip around the elastic so that the knot is inside the object.

3RD VARIATION

EAR LOOP FACE MASK SEWING

Free latex operating mask with bias tapestry

This option does not use elastics and therefore, if you have not an option, it is a great option.

-- quilting cotton fabric, high-quality tissue is the best

– double fold 1/2 ″ pretty tape (or handmade binding), two 35 ″ tissue masking pattern

Tie the top and bottom two squares together, leaving the faces open.

Turn and press well. Press well

Pleat the textile according to the pattern component (or, if desired, all in one direction).

Enclose raw side edges with the middle of the bias tape. Break the bias tape together into the center of the sandwich mask. Connection ends in small knots of bias tape.

All homemade masks must have an enclosed pocket to bring in a filter. At present, no changes are allowed for the mask unless there is a low supply of a certain material used to produce them.

Face Mack With Filter Pocket And Adjustable

Considerations:

Re-wash cotton before you start seeing, the factory is made of cotton or cotton / poly strong wavy and when washed in hot water, it does not leak.

Product Size Width Bias or 2 "width bias fabric 2 * * * * *

Plastic Twist Tie or * * pipe cleaner**1 About 6,5" *

* Based on input and Community requests these instructions have been updated * *

Serge or zigzag the short edges of your rectangle.

Fold the right sides of your fabric, matching the short borders.

Mark 1.5 "in either hand unfinished.

Stitch the seam to the mark around your finished bottom, reversing it at the beginning and end of your line. Click the opening of your seam quota.

Topstitch the bottom, 1/8 "from the fold of your seam allowance.

Label 1/2 "above your seam allowance's unstitched hand. Fold the label on your face. Press flat. Press flat. Topstitch about 1/8 "edge of the entire mask.

Relevant twist tie info: do not use wrapped paper ties (such as bread ties). The paper is washed away and waded and the metal content is clean.

-- Your twist tie on top of the mask (top the unfinished edge of the pocket). Stitch the twist tie around the top edge of the pocket opening.

Fold your mask 3/4 "folds * * so folds facing down on the front of the mask*

* Draw a stitch on the mask's edge to secure the platters.

* * Lay your bias tape or 2 "fabric strap around the right sides on the bottom of the mask. Have the 12 "inclination band hanging below the mask and the rest above the mask.

Split in a 3/8 "seam allowance***

Fold the bias band's raw edge in order to match the mask's raw edge. Hold the folded edges bound together and cover your past stitching on the mask. Stitch the entire length of the blazing tape.

* For elastic ear bends, 1/4 "elastic 2 parts 12" long 1/2 "bias or 2" wide 2 parts 6 "long

Put the bias strip together on the edge of the mask or 2" fabric strip right side. Leave 1⁄2 "above and cut the surplus to 1⁄2" below the mask. Fold the 1⁄2 "overhang on top and bottom to the back of the mask. Stitch in place with a 3⁄8 "seam supply.

Fold the raw edge of your prejudice to suit your mask's raw edge. Fold it again to cover the previous stitching with a folded bottom and the topstitch in place.

Connect your elastic into the bias tape tube. Fastening ends and fastening knot within the tape tube. Done! Done!

APPROVED SUBSTITUTIONS:

You can now use 1/4" fabric ties, 1/4" par chord and 1/4" decorative elastic instead of elastic ear loops.

Many types of elastic are available in 1" and 1/2" and are readily cut and not sprayable in our tests.

You can now use pipe cleaners or flower wire instead of plastic ties.

CHAPTER 5: DIY Face Masks Usage

In view of the virus pandemic, face masks are currently in great demand. There is a need for millions of masks and you can help. On Saturday's request to resolve a national lack of facial masks, the White House could not say when more health workers in the country would have more safe masks.

If you have a sewing machine, you can help in this one way. (We have no-sew mask instructions, too, if you cannot sew.) Now, CDC suggests that everyone wear masks in public.

In view of the shortage of face masks in the medical profession, it is our duty to take responsibility for such supplies.

The World Health Organization has previously advised you to wear a mask only if you care about a person who is suspected about VIRUS or if you cough or sneeze. The CDC also, however, revised its advice to allow people to wear face masks in public.

WHO reminds us that masks only work when used in conjunction with frequent and proper washing of hands.

So if you wear a mask, you need to learn how to use it to get it right.

Below are guides for personal use masks (first section) and hospital donations (second section).

Two types of face masks will reduce the chances of having virus: operational facial masks and breathers, the latter also known as N-95 masks.

The news is about surgical face masks and what surgeons, dentists and nurses generally use for the care of patients. They are fairly loose and thin, so tiny droplets can still pass through the mask's parts and are not inherently foolproof.

Then there are breathers, often used by builders but also by doctors seeing patients with VIRUS. We are heavy-duty and shapely to the nose. These masks remove about 95% of airborne contaminants, including viruses and bacteria, according to the CDC.

The Centers for Disease Control and Prevention states that DIY masks should be rendered last resort in times of crisis and "ideally used in connection with the face shield covering the entire forehead and sides of the face (that extends to the chin or below

1. If you wish to take the additional precautions of wearing a facial mask, make a mask for yourself – do not buy one and contribute to the shortage.

2. If you are sewing expert and would like to support your local hospitals, you can make large quantities of face masks in your home. Clear standards need to be met to make them medically permissible, so be sure to obey them. If not, your job can be for nothing.

Although home-made masks may not be of medical quality, the CDC considers well-made masks, like the ones below, useful. It is also better to visit the hospital in advance and see if they accept donations-some hospitals do not even allow donations of personal protective equipment, while others have comprehensive facial mask requirements.

CHAPTER 6: Medical Protective Masks (AKA N95, KN95 Masks)

What is a N95 Respirator Mask?

Respiratory masks have received increased attention since late, although they have long been used for other purposes, including occupational health. N95 refers to the rating given to masks that meet the required minimum requirements for the transmission of particles by the National Institute for occupational safety and health (NIOSH).

The N95 respirator mask is designed for filtering up to 95% of airborne particles 0.3 microns or larger which may otherwise penetrate directly into the wearer's nose and mouth.

These masks can also be used by people with an infectious disease in order to prevent bacteria from entering the user's nose and mouth and endangering others. Although these masks do not protect against 100 percent particulate transmission, they do help prevent infection spread.

N95 masks can be bought without a valve to make breathing easier. The optimum protection is achieved if the respiratory mask snugly fits into the face and protects the nose and mouth without leaving empty spaces on the bottom. Air masks should be properly fitted to the wearer and should not be obstructed by facial or jewelry fur.

Respirator masks, used in industrial and health care facilities, are commonly used for occupational safety. The workplace masks used must be NIOSH-approved, meaning that they meet the minimum requirements defined by the National Institute for Safety and Health.

When purchasing respiratory masks, the intended purpose should be taken into account. Various types are designed for particular purposes and provide various levels of security. Another problem is that the mask contains latex, which is an irritation for others. There are latex free breathing masks N95 and they are labeled as such.

You may be in a position with a high risk of inhaling chemicals or fumes which are extremely harmful and dangerous to your health. You may be exposed to substances such as blood-borne or airborne pathogens that ensure that your employees are safe.

In fact, there is a law that tells you to protect your employees. Many companies claim to have healthy facial masks, but it is better to choose items that have the approval seal from the National Institute for Occupational Safety or the Administration of Food and Drugs.

These are your strongest assurance that your masks actually prevent you from contracting any pathogens in your vicinity.

You certainly want your workplace and your employees to be safe. It is best to ensure that your protection is assured when you are operating. The N95 mask is a very secure type of mask for your employees.

With great manufacturing efficiency, these masks will ensure the health of your workers. You do not need to have one type of mask, but you have a range of versions, as such masks are designed for various industries that may have special requirements.

When you heard of portable respiratory machines, they are no different from the N95 masks. You can filter and block soil, coal, iron ore, flour and dust. You can be confident that other related materials can also be blocked.

You can also be sure that diseases such as influenza and tuberculosis can be avoided if you correctly use these disposable respirators. For a disposable respirator, you would have the additional advantage in that you have a built-in respirator. It is more than a basic mask, you can be assured you have a good amount of oxygen.

You might be interested in those, but you need to be wary of the price tag. However, you do not have to worry too much because when you order a mask from a manufacturer in bulk, you will definitely hit your price goals. And all of these lightweight respirators and N95 masks are well within the price range to help you sleep better at night.

The N95 is the most common series of particulate breathing masks, which comply with US government standards. The face masks are tested to reduce exposure of NIOSH, the National Institute for Safety and Health, to airborne contaminants.

CHAPTER 7: DIY Fabric Face Masks Requirements

Medical facial masks are incomplete. Hospitals need face masks urgently for medical professionals. You can use your time and talents to make your home better when you sew fabric facial masks and donate them to your local hospital while you sit at home during this insane time.

Fabric facial masks do not replace medical facial masks. However, due to the shortage, many hospitals only use them or are coated with a medical grade mask in non-critical areas of the hospital.

The CDC now wants people to wear cloth masks as they leave for their simple orders, such as food shopping. This means that for every member of your family, you should make many masks. DO NOT use N-95 or masks of medical quality. Save those for health workers who are in direct contact with the patients affected.

In summary, the face masks will comply with these requirements:

— fit snugly but securely against the side of the face

— be securing them with ties or ear-loops

— Have several layers of fabric

— Allow for ventilation without restriction

Here are a few feedback that I hope will be useful.

1. They must be slightly wider (more upright!) so that they can stretch from above the nose to under the chin.
2. If you can adjust the size of the ones you make, this is helpful. Many nurses have very small ears. So growing scale up and down your pattern, so if you can, you have medium and high.
3. The masks he had were elastic and wrapped over his head. These have several suit constraints. When you can make ties behind the eyes, more people can suit.
They are not helpful without a good fit.
You people do this — we thank your efforts! In certain cases the documents are approved ONE single face mask per day. My husband's has been stretched out within 3 hours and it is useless (the N95 mask) and handmade masks are perfect substitutes. (And they have to be washable to reuse).
Most of the mask designs I am seeing are the same size: 6"x9 "so that doctors and nurses can pick one that suits them best.
Call your local hospital before you start sewing, to see if they accept donations of tissue masks to find out whether they have particular specifications.
Face masks should be made of high quality, 100 percent cotton tightly woven material. You can use a few other things when you have no quilter fabric at home: T-Shirts Cotton Pillowcases or Bandanas (not microfiber).

CHAPTER 8: Fabric Face Mask Patterns

Face Mask With Elastic Loops

It is the most common design on the medical face with two elastic loops slipping over the ore. You can also manage this pattern even though you are a beginner. I recommend that you add an additional inch or two to boost the cover of this mask.

This mask includes side elastic earrings, but the fabric is cut into ergonomic shape that fits comfortably over the nose rather than into a folding mask. It also has a pocket to insert a medical mask into it. This design is also available in various sizes for children and adults.

This mask has a contrasting trim around the two external edges, which gives the mask a pleasant finish and would possibly help keep the elastic secure. The tutorial even has big step-by-step photos.

Basic Pleated Mask

This is the same basic mask as # 1, but it is interesting to hear the two different ways things clarified.

Face Mask With Ties

Manufactured face masks with ties, developed by a nurse, this design requires no elasticity. Nurses claim they prefer tying masks because for longer periods they are flexible rather than elastic and easier to wear.

This mask will likely be most convenient for medical professionals to use, as it incorporates a flexible wire in its nose that helps to preserve its form and bias connections to make it fit.

Cricut Face Mask
Save time and use your Cricut Maker to cut out pattern pieces.

Face Mask with Filter Pocket
This design and mask tutorial has a filter pocket and has fabric connections rather than elasticity. Once done, the mask is three layers, even without a filter.
No Sew T-Shirt Face Mask
Transform a T-shirt to a face mask with a few cuts. Ultimately, this is a brilliant process!

Hair T-Shirt Face Mask
Transforming a t-shirt into a facial mask using a hair elasticity and safety pin. I do not suggest using any filter material for children as children may not be fully conscious of their consumption of oxygen. I always recommend that you should not take your children in public unless it is absolutely necessary.
Any of the above mask patterns can be re-sized to suit babies. That said, here are some common patterns for children.

Classic Olson Face Mask

This is the classic Olson Face Mask for children with a height. It is a fitted, elastic-bonded mask.

This mask is appropriately suited to a child; it has gathered sides and uses corded elastic to become smoother on small ears.

Recall that it is necessary to stay at home to slow the spread of VIRUS. When you need to take drastic action, wear a mask and follow measures to hold 6 feet apart.

CHAPTER 9: How To Sew A Surgical Face Mask

Several manufacturers demanded a blueprint for making handmade surgical masks for hospitals and their populations. The DIY design in this post teaches you to create a tissue plunged face mask with elastic earrings or fabric links.

The cloth face mask can be made with an inner pocket where additional filter material can be added.

Whether you cannot find elastic earrings or do not want to use them, there are additional instructions for creating and using fabric band. You may make fabric bonds from cotton cloth, t-shirts, or use ready-made binding tools.

Are Fabric Face Masks necessary?

The supply of surgical masks is currently at a critical all-time low across the country. Regular disposable masks in hospitals are ordered back and there is a strong demand for healthcare workers safety equipment.

According to the CDC, cloth masks are an alternative for disaster response if other supplies are exhausted. Due to these issues, a number of hospitals across the world have demanded handmade surgical masks to be used as an emergency s measure.

However, federal health officials are also suggesting that people cover their noses and mouths with cloth-faced masks in public.

It is a voluntary initiative for public safety that is intended to help avoid spreading when people have to visit public places and public transit stations.

In addition, CDC encourages the use of plain cloth face coverings to slow down the transmission of the virus and to protect people who have the virus and who do not know how to pass it on to others.

Sewing a face mask will require surgical masks and N95 masks in medical grades to be reserved for health workers and patients.

A big difference

Homemade face mask is not as effective as the CDC suggested filtration mask N95 and is not a replacement for a proper EPI. Rather, it is intended to respond to emergency backup masks requests from the hospitals.

To support community members "slow the spread" in public settings, in which it is difficult to sustain certain social distance interventions.

The Centers for Disease Control and Prevention (CDC) has clarified that handmade masks are approved as a last resort in case of crisis.

HCP can use home-made masks (e.g., bandana, scarf) as a last resort for patients with VIRUS where the face masks are not available. Home-made masks are, however, not recognized as PPE since their ability to protect HCP is uncertain.

Caution should be taken when this choice is considered. Homemade masks are best to be used in conjunction with a facial shield covering the whole front (which reaches up or down to the chin) and facial sides.

Many hospitals and clinics accept home-made mask donations. Organizations like Masks for Heroes provide a searchable database of donation seekers. When you wonder where masks can be donated, they can help you to locate a hospital or clinic that needs them.

Before spending time stitching a big batch of masks, call first to ask if they recognize them. If this design (2 layers of fabric with a pocket for extra disposable inserts) suits your requirements, please ask. You may also inquire about the method of drop-off / pick-up.

A broad variety of household materials were tested for use in home-crafted masks by researchers from Cambridge University. We assessed how well household materials could absorb small particles and filter them.

Test results indicate that cotton t-shirts, pillowcases or other cotton fabrics are the best choice for DIY fabric masks. The application of a double layer of material for your DIY mask increases the efficacy of filtration slightly.

CHAPTER 10: Steps For Sewing A Fabric Hospital Mask

DIY Surgical Mask Design

The finished adult mask will be 7.75'' long and 3.75'' tall.

1/8'' flat elastic for earrings (with tight weaves) or 4 fabric bindings (the same cotton fabric can be employed in making strips, binding or using cotton jersey strips) fabric scissor rulers or clips sewing machine and thread

Cut List

To an adult size machine:

Cut 1 fabric rectangle 16'' long and 8.5'' wide Cut 2 piece.

Fold the long sides in the middle and fold them in half to enclose the raw edges down the rectangle length on the edge to create the relations.

Step 1:

Sew to the rim, with pocket Fold the fabric rectangle into half, facing each other on the right side.

Sew along the top 8.5'' width edge with a wide 5/8'' seam supply. Leave a 3 "opening in the middle of this seam to create a filter pocket gap, so that after stitching, the mask can be turned correctly.

Operational mask sewing materials and supplies Do you want a filter pocket?

It is totally okay if you do not want or need a pocket. You still have to leave a gap so you can turn the mask correctly. After you have attached the elastic or knots (in the next step) and turned the mask out to the right, the opening can be closed. Then the rest of the directions can be followed.

Sewing the seam for the filter pocket in the surgical mask of a fabric Next turn the fabric in the middle of a side so that the seam with the pocket opening is oriented. Push the seam open with an iron.

Fold the excess seam allowance below, covering the fabric's raw edge. Topstitch or zig-zag point to finish the edge on either side of the surface. It helps to prevent the fabric from fraying when any filters are added and removed.

Step 2:

Elastic pine or cloth bond: Pin one piece of elastic on each side of the mask, one end at the top corner and one at the bottom end of the fabric rectangle. This produces the ear loop when the mask is turned right and folded out. Place the ends of the elastic on top and bottom of the fabric roughly 1/4.

The elastic component itself is sandwiched between the two fabric layers. When you turn out the mask to the right, the elastic is on the outside.

Repeat this process for two ear loops on each side.

Fabric pinned ties to the cloth mask fabric or to the mask elastic before sewing Alternative

– Use fabric bonds: if you cannot find elastic bands, or prefer to use fabric bonds, you can use 4 fabric bonds, one at each corner. Each tie will have a length of 18″. Open one tie in each corner to avoid links in the side seams.

You can also use twill tape, twisted tape or cotton jersey strips (t-shirt material).

The finished mask is then worn by adding the strips behind the eyes. See notes at the end of the chapter.

Step 3:

Sew the sides, sew each side of the facemask, sew the ties with a seam allowance of 3/8″. Backstitch the elastic or cloth bindings to protect them. Trim the corners with scissors so that the mask can be turned out more quickly on the right. You should not cut the stitches unintentionally.

Turn the mask out on the right side and click the hammer. You may use a crayon to push the corners out.

Using wire on a fabric mask, to create a flexible nose piece Optional: insert a flexible nose piece Cut 6-inch of a floral wire, pipe cleaner, or any other flexible wire for nose piece creation. I plied the ends of the wire to keep them from sticking through the cloth. Place the wire in the pocket hole and slide it to the top of the mask. Stitch it around on all three sides to preserve it.

Step 4:

Making the folds for a face mask

Make the platters make the mask with three lines that are evenly distant. To do this, you can use a water soluble fabric pen to measure and mark. Alternatively, you can do what I have done, fold the mask in thirds-fold the sides down in the middle and fold in half again using iron to make a plump.

Using pins to lock three folds on the surgical mask to make three 1/2 "evenly spaced platters. Use your markings. Pin down the folds; make sure all the folds face the same way. Open the sides of the plates to protect them. I just like stitching the sides twice to make sure.

Once the mask is worn, the plates will open downwards so that no particles accumulate in the folding pockets.

Place stitching down on the side of the surgical mask fabric in hospitals Pattern troubleshooting What if you do not find elastic?

I learned from a lot of people who find it difficult to find elastic. If you cannot find elastic for earrings, then you can make a mask with fabric bonds.

To tie fabric links: cut 18″ long fabric strips, 1.75″ length. Fold the long side so they meet in the middle (longitudinal or hot-dog style).

Fold the strips again in half (lengthwise) to accommodate the raw edges. Stitch the strips to build the ties along the bottom.

If you wanted these straps to have a bit of stretch, you could also cut long strips from cotton jersey or knit T- material. The great thing about using jersey fabric is that it will form itself into a tube when you stretch it. And, it's comfortable to wear since it keeps a bit of stretch.

Whichever option you choose, you'll want to cut 4 pieces about 18" long, and attach one strip to each of the corners. The mask will fasten by tying the straps behind the head.

What about metal to help the mask fit better?

To help the mask fit better around your nose, you can insert a length of flexible metal to the top inside of the mask, through the pocket insert opening before forming the pleats. Then, you can topstitch down around the metal insert so that it stays in place. I've seen people use pipe cleaners, floral wire, or twist ties.

What can you use as a filter?

It is so important that everyone understands that while wearing a cloth face mask can offer some level of protection, it can't protect against viruses the same way that an N95 mask can.

Many different types of filters have been suggested, like coffee filters, felt, and vacuum filter bags. Not all of these filters are effective, and not all of them are safe.

Without further research into the safety and efficacy of face mask filter materials, we won't know what the best filter is.

Face Mask Filter Materials: Pros and Cons HEPA filters.

In testing, a layer of HEPA vacuum cleaner bag seemed to perform the best.

Nonetheless, it is difficult to breathe through. In addition, several people have raised concerns about the health of materials (like fiberglass) used to manufacture such filters. At this time I can't suggest them.

Coffee filters.

Some of the mask prototypes that the CDC has released contains a layer of a coffee filter. They are easily available and usable.

Black store towels.

Others have tested the effectiveness of blue shop towels, including these. They look good, but the data hasn't been released publically or confirmed.

Dryer pad or baby wipes.

Since these products are covered in fragrances and other chemicals, I don't suggest using these as a filter.

Non- interfacing.

It has been mentioned several times in the articles. I can't find evidence saying it would help. When you want to use interfacing, avoid the fusible / iron-on forms.

Flannel

These materials are not as similar as the cotton fabric on the outside of the mask, so it is unlikely that they would make the filtration more effective. They can also trap moisture.

Another cotton fabric sheet

Research indicates that cotton t-shirt material or tightly woven cotton fabric are the most secure and convenient choice for a filter.

CHAPTER 11: Homemade Facemask Patterns

Please use tightly woven fabric, such as a quilting thread, to make a homemade face mask. Please also be sure to heat / highly dry and wash your textile before you cut pieces and start sewing. Before handling your clean materials or sewing, make sure to wash your hands.

Recall testing and verifying if the company you are sewing needs a certain pattern. If not, you can use one of the following patterns:

NOTE: It was very difficult at this point to find elastic, so I marked * with the patterns underneath that use straps instead of elastic. Most designs use biased strap tape. You can buy bias tape, but it is actually very easy to make your own of the same fabric you use to make the mask (and this is better because it is 100% cotton).

* Belt Pattern Mask

It uses belts instead of elastic, has a pocket to attach a filter and contains (optional) nasal wire. This seems like a Really GOOD model choice.

This face mask model was developed by the Turban Project and was shared by Deaconess Health Systems in their call for people to make masks.

This mask is incredibly simple to make – it starts with a tissue rectangle that is folded to resemble a surgical mask with elastic circling the face. If you have a sewing background, you can probably do each in about 15 minutes.

* Sweet Red Pappy Bias Tape Mask

This pattern is a great alternative because it uses biased tape straps, rather than elastic, which have become difficult to find. This pattern is a great option. It is the same general design as the Deaconess mask but also contains a pocket that can be inserted by the healthcare provider. This mask is very similar to the deaconess mask and is also pretty straightforward to create.

* Fu Face Mask

This is yet another simple mask design – I have sewn up a couple of these now and will soon add a photo. This one has no plates, but is angled to provide good face coverage. The Fu Face Mask uses bias tape or tape for binding, so if you find it difficult to find elastic it is a good choice.

* A.B. Face mask

This facial mask was designed and shared by Jessica Nandino. It has plates in the front and links on the top of the head and on the bottom of the back.

This pattern takes a little more time to construct due to the connection of the ties, but also to the strong, comfortable fit. AND it has been designed to fit over a N95 mask and probably prolong their life.

This mask pattern is available in 4 sizes and uses elastic hair ties to go over the ears. The mask pattern is made in 4 sizes. It uses a contoured fit over the nose instead of platelets.

CHAPTER 12: When Are You Supposed To Wear A Face Mask?

The World Health Organization (WHO-Trust Source) recommends that you wear a mask only if you:

Have a fever, cough, or other respiratory symptoms, but look after someone with a disease of the breath. In this case, wear a mask if you are within 6 feet or nearer to the person who is ill.

This is because surgical masks: do not remove smaller particles from the air do not fit snugly on the face, so airborne particles can leaking in the mask's sides Some studies have been unable to prove that surgical masks effectively prevent exposure in group or public spaces to infectious diseases.

The Reliable Source Centers for Disease Control and Prevention (CDC) officially does not prescribe the use of surgical masks or N95 respirators to the general public in order to protect against respiratory diseases like VIRUS.

In the case of VIRUS, however, the CDC advises the public at large to wear cloth facial covers to prevent disease transmission. The CDC also gives instructions on how to create your own.

How To Put On A Surgical Mask

If you need to wear a surgical mask, take the following steps to correctly wear it.

Steps To Put On A Facial Mask

Wash your hands with soap and water for at least 20 seconds or rub your hands thoroughly with an alcohol-based hand sanitizer.
Check for facial mask defects like tears or broken loops.
Put the colored side of the mask to the outside.
When present, make sure that the metal strip is at the top of the mask and positioned against your nose bridge.
If the mask has the ear loops, then hold the mask with both loops and place a loop on each ear.

Ties: Keep the upper strings of the mask.
Tie the top strings in a secure bow below your head's crown.
Keep the lower strings tight in a bow close to your neck.
Dual elastic bands:
Pull over your head the top band and place it against your head's crown. Pull the bottom band over your head and set it against your back.
Place and pinch the bendable metallic upper strip into your nose form and press with your fingertips.
Bring the mouth and nose to the bottom of the mask.
Ensure sure that the mask suits perfectly.
When in place, do not touch the mask.
If the mask is soiled or wet, swap it with a new mask.

What Not To Do When Wearing A Surgical Mask

There are a variety of steps to be taken after the mask is properly worn to avoid the movement of pathogens onto the face or hands.

Do not:

Touch the mask until the mask is fixed on your face, as pathogens may move from the ear,

Hang the mask around your neck,

Reuse single-use masks if you have to touch the face mask while wearing it, first wash your hands. Make sure to wash your hands or use a hand sanitizer afterwards as well.

How To Remove A Surgical Mask

It is vital that the face mask is removed properly to ensure that no germs are passed to your hand or face. You do want to make sure that you securely remove the mask.

Steps to remove a mask

Wash your hands well or use a hand sanitizer before taking the mask off.

Stop touching the mask itself, because it could be dirty. Keep it only by loops, links or bands.

Remove the mask carefully from your face until you: first unhook the ear loops, unload the bottom loop or then remove the bottom band by raising it over the head and do the same with the top band Holding the mask loops, tie or strings.

Wash your hands thoroughly or use a hand sanitizer after removing the mask.

CONCLUSION

The CDC (Center for Disease Control) estimates that 1.7 million people are infected with hospital-related infections, with about 1% dying annually, around 100,000 people dying due to hospital-related infections.

This number is rather troubling, cause for change, and the use of disposable materials, in particular single-use disposable materials, is a way to minimize this amount.

When you are a health care provider, it is strongly recommended that you become a good example of protecting yourself and your patients by wearing these items. You should play your part in avoiding germ spread and defend yourself from fluid splatters.

You can wear a full mask or a half mask, depending on what you have to do. You can spice up your masks and choose the most enjoyable, cartoon-type masks with their designs too. These are not made of rubber or fiberglass, which makes it very easy to breathe.

Many of the items you need are for single use only, medical facial masks, gloves, etc. You can make use of protective gloves in the operations procedures most of the time. These gloves typically consist of cotton, nylon, neoprene and rubber nitrile. However, many people are prone and uncomfortable with latex and prefer gloves made from a different material.

Then you have the choice of strength or cornstarch lubricating the gloves. Some days, you can ask for gloves that are tailored to your side, so that you can understand more clearly the equipment you are going to use for surgery.

As a healthcare professional, many medical and dental devices are available which only have to be used once. This is critical if patients and healthcare workers are not to be exposed to infectious diseases. The dentist usually uses medical face masks and test gloves for every patient once.

A wide selection of face masks can be chosen, making them ear-loops, anti-fogs, ties, cones, shapes or full face masks types. You can limit your options according to the price range you prefer.

With the difficult environment, some of these disposable items can only be expensive to use once, such as test gloves and medical masks. It is therefore necessary to ensure that you have a thorough analysis of the type you want, and that they are likely to be within your price line.

You would definitely want to limit your range approved by the Food and Drug Administration and the National Institute for Job Health, so that your masks are of high quality.

Made in the USA
San Bernardino, CA
02 May 2020